Welcome

1  Number the pictures in order.

a

b

c

d

2 Match.

1

2

a Everyone's got tickilitis.

b Please come to Space Island.

c Have you got a tifftiff plant?

d Oh, no!

3 Number the pictures in order.

Come on, Kim, Katy!

Ah! This is the problem!

Hurray!

Quick! Quick!

Goodbye, Earth!

20... 19... 18...

4 Look at Activity 3 and write.

| Ah   Quick   19   Kim   Goodbye   Hurray |

a   Come on, _____, Katy!

b   _____! This is the problem!

c   _____!

d   Quick! _____!

e   _____, Earth!

f   20 ... _____ ... 18 ...

5 Match.

1
2
3
4
5
6

a. My name's Katy.

b. Hello. I'm Captain Conrad.

c. I'm PROD 1.

d. I'm President Pop. Welcome to Space Island.

e. Hello, I'm PROD 2.

f. I'm Kim.

6 Draw yourself. Then write.

Hello.

My name's _____.

I'm (age) _____.

7 Listen and write. Then draw lines.

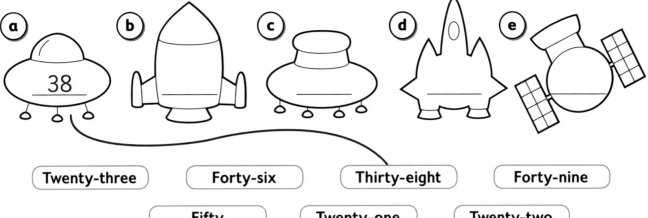

a   38

b

c

d

e

Twenty-three   Forty-six   Thirty-eight   Forty-nine

Fifty   Twenty-one   Twenty-two

Thirty-seven   Forty-four   Thirty-five

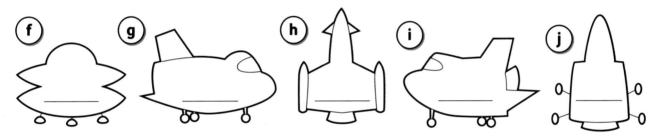

f

g

h

i

j

 **8** Write and say.

a	21	24	27	30	33
b	33	35	37		41
c	20			35	40
d	10	20	30		
e			39	44	49
f	18	20			26

9 **Listen, write and match.**

1  Boris   <u>Wednesday</u>   **a**

2  Billy   _____   **b**

3  Jenny   _____   **c**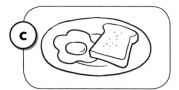

4  Marie   _____   **d**

5  Andy   _____   **e**

6  Mike   _____   **f**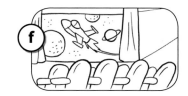

7  Judy   _____   **g**

10  **What's your favourite day? Write.**

_____ favourite day?

My _____
is _____.

Lesson 4

6

11   **Listen and circle the correct days.**

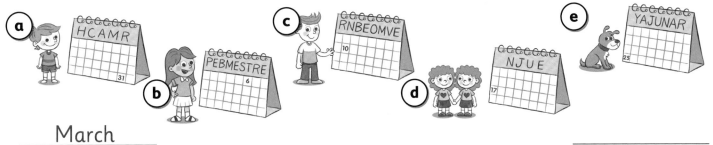

|	AUGUST					
Sunday	Monday	Tuesday	Wednesday	Thursday	Friday	Saturday
	(1st)	2nd	3rd	4th	5th	6th
7th	8th	9th	10th	11th	12th	13th
14th	15th	16th	17th	18th	19th	20th
21st	22nd	23rd	24th	25th	26th	27th
28th	29th	30th	31st			

12 **Unscramble and write the months.**

a HCAMR

b PEBMESTRE 6

c RNBEOMVE 10

d NJUE 17

e YAJUNAR 25

March _____

_____   _____

_____   _____

13 **Look at Activity 12 and write.**

① When were you born?

I was born on the __6th_____ .

② Were you born in December?

No, _____ . I _____
_____ .

1 Write. Then colour.

flowers   sun   insects   birds   mushrooms
~~clouds~~   pond   rock   animal   trees

1 ___clouds___

2 _____

3 _____

4 _____

5 _____

6 _____

7 _____

8 _____

9 _____

10 _____

2   **Listen, colour and draw.**

3 **Look at Activity 2 and write.**

1 How many ponds are there? There's ___one blue pond___ .

2 How many flowers are there? There are _____.

3 How many rocks are there? _____ brown _____.

4 How many birds are there? _____ blue _____.

5 How many insects are there? _____.

6 How many animals are there? _____.

4   **Look and write.**

| ants | butterflies | rainbow | roses | sky | spiders | ~~wind~~ | worms |

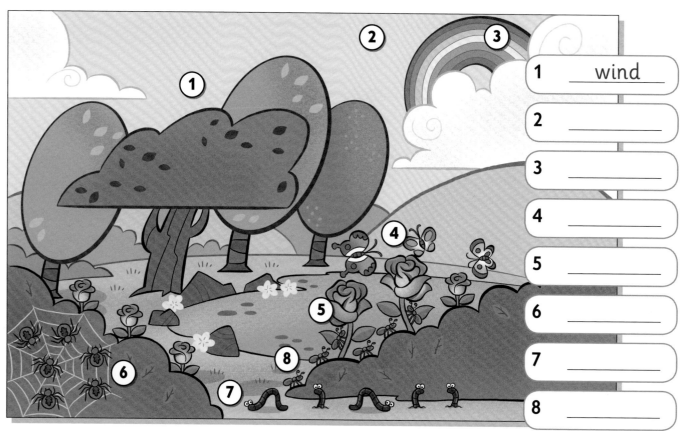

1   wind

2   _____

3   _____

4   _____

5   _____

6   _____

7   _____

8   _____

5 **Look at Activity 4 and write.**

a   There __are__ __six__ ants.

b   There _____ _____ rainbow.

c   There _____ _____ worms.

d   There _____ _____ butterflies.

e   There _____ _____ roses.

f   _____ _____ _____ spiders.

g   _____ _____ _____ trees.

h   _____ _____ _____ clouds.

6 **Read. Then draw and colour.**

There is a big blue pond. There are three green trees.

There are some pink insects. There are four yellow birds.

There is a rainbow. There aren't any butterflies. There isn't any wind.

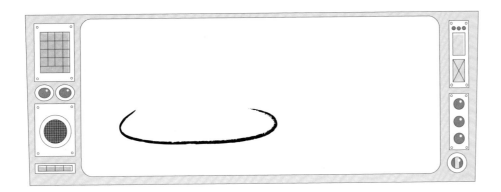

7 **Listen and tick (✓).**
1:29

1

a b ✓

2
a b

3
a b

4
a b

8 **Unscramble and write.**

1 they / are / where   <u>Where are they</u>   ?

2 the / park / at   _____ .

3 is / where / he   _____ ?

4 museum / the / at   _____ .

9 **Read the story again. Where is the tifftiff plant?**

Write. In the _____.

10 **Find the mistakes and write.**

1 There are two mushrooms. <u>There are three mushrooms</u> .

2 There are some birds. _____.

3 There's a flower. _____.

4 There aren't any worms. _____.

5 There's a rock. _____.

11 **Number the pictures in order.**

12 Read the words. Circle the pictures.

~~chair~~   hair   pair   tear

13 Listen and connect the letters. Then write.

1	t	i	p	s ____ ____
2	r	a	t	r ____ ____
3	s	e	ll	t _a_ _p_
4	sh	a	ch	sh ____ ____

14 Listen and write the words.

1 _f_ _air_   2 ___ ___   3 ___ ___   4 ___ ___

15 Read aloud. Then listen and check.

There's a boy on the bed. There's a tear near his hair. There's a pair of socks near the chair.

Wider World

16 **Read and write T = True or F = False.**

1   Pablo and Lucy live in Spain.   `F`

2   Lucy plays board games on weekends.   ☐

3   Pablo makes sandcastles in the summer.   ☐

4   Lucy lives in a city.   ☐

17   **Look, read and tick (✓).**

Where do you play?

① In the playground

② On the beach

③ At home

18  **Choose someone from Activity 17. Imagine and write.**

I'm _____ .

I'm from _____ .

I live _____ .

I play _____ .

19 **Look and draw. Then write.**

1  + | = 6

2  – | = 4

3 + | = 7

4  – | = 2

1 Four insects plus ___two insects___ equals six.

2 Seven mushrooms minus _____ equals four.

3 Four clouds plus _____ equals seven.

4 Six flowers minus _____ equals two.

20 **Read and write.**

1 There are three birds plus one spider. How many legs are there? ___14___

2 There are two ants plus one worm. How many legs are there? _____

3 There are two birds plus three horses. How many legs are there? _____

4 There are two dogs plus three snakes. How many legs are there? _____

21 **Write the numbers.**

1 eleven + ___two___ = thirteen

2 twenty – _____ = thirteen

3 twelve + _____ = thirteen

4 eighteen – _____ = thirteen

Lesson 9

22   **Look and write.**

Crossword grid:
- 1 Down: T R E E S

23   **Look and write.**

There's ...

1 _____a rock_____.

2 _____.

3 _____.

There are some ...

4 _____.

5 _____.

6 _____.

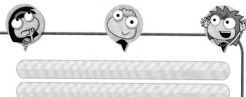

I CAN

I can recognise nature words.
I can ask and answer about how many there are.
I can do simple sums and number puzzles.

24 **Look and write.**

I play at the park.

1

Are there _____
_____ insects ___ at the park?

Yes, there are _____
in the tree.

2

How many _____
are on the rock?

_____ one
_____ .

3

Is there any wind or rain?

No, _____
_____ .

25 **Write about your favourite place.**

My favourite place is _____.

There's _____. There are _____.

There isn't _____. There aren't _____.

2 Me

1 **Listen and colour. Then match.**

small nose   blue eyes

white moustache ──────── (Grandad)   small glasses

short beard ────────────   red hair

                        (Mum)

green eyes   (Peter)   grey hair

blond hair   thick eyebrows

2 **Look at Activity 1 and write.**

1 Grandad has got a short ___beard___, a _____ moustache and _____ eyebrows.

2 Mum has got blond _____ and a _____ nose.

3 Peter _____ a small nose and _____ hair.

4 Grandad _____ grey hair, green _____ and small _____.

5 Mum and Peter have got _____.

3 **Choose, draw and colour. Then write.**

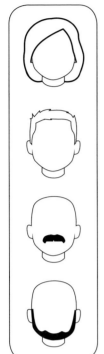  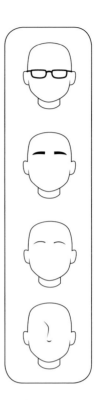

I've got _____ and _____.

I haven't got _____.

4 **Look and write.**

| He's got | He hasn't got | She's got | She hasn't got |

1 __He's got__ thick eyebrows.   **5** _____ a small nose.

2 _____ long hair.   **6** _____ long hair.

3 _____ glasses.   **7** _____ glasses.

4 _____ a beard.   **8** _____ blond hair.

5 **Listen and number.**

a **John**	b **Mary**	c **Tom**	d **Sally**
 **1**			

6 **Look at Activity 5 and write.**

strong arms   strong legs   long eyelashes
long neck   round chin   ~~short fingernails~~

a John hasn't got _short fingernails_____.

b Mary has got a _____.

c Tom has got _____.
He hasn't got _____.

d Sally has got a _____.
She hasn't got _____.

7 **Write about your family.**

1 _____ has got _____.
_____ hasn't got _____.

2 _____ has got _____.
_____ hasn't got _____.

3 _____ has got _____.
_____ hasn't got _____.

8 Listen and tick (✓). Then write.

1

2

3

He's got _____ hair and _____ arms. He hasn't got _____.

9 **Read. Then write.**

> My name's Meesoo. I'm 10 years old. I love swimming and dancing. I've got black hair and thin eyebrows. I've got strong arms and legs. I've got a flat stomach. I haven't got broad shoulders. I haven't got glasses.

1 Has she got blond hair? _No, she hasn't_____.

2 Has she got thin eyebrows? _____.

3 Has she got strong legs and arms? _____.

4 Has she got glasses? _____.

5 Has she got broad shoulders? _____.

10  **Write about a friend.**

Friend's name: _____

1 Has _____ got glasses? _____.

2 _____? No, _____ hasn't.

3 _____? Yes, _____ has.

11 **Read the story again. Has Dr Bones got a white beard?**

Write. _____ .

12 **Read the sentences and write *T = True* or *F = False*.**

1 Dr Bones has got a moustache. ☐

2 She's got long blond hair. ☐

3 She hasn't got glasses. ☐

4 She hasn't got tickilitis. ☐

13 **Number the pictures in order.**

a — We've got Dr Bones! ☐

b — Everyone on the bus has got tickilitis. ☐

c — And she's got a white beard. ☐

d — Dr Bones is on the bus. ☐

e — She's got blond hair. ☐

14 **Find the mistakes and write.**

1 Dr Bones has got a tifftiff plant.   <u>Dr Bones hasn't got a tifftiff plant</u> .

2 Kate and Kim have got tickilitis.   _____ .

3 Dr Bones hasn't got glasses and spots.   _____ .

15 **Read the words. Circle the pictures.**

ay er

say dinner letter play

16 **Listen and connect the letters. Then write.**

1 d — i — d   p ___ _____

2 s — a — s   th ___ ___

3 p — a — t   d _a_ _d_

4 th — i — th   s ___ ___

17 **Listen and write the words.**

1 _s_ _ay_   2 ___ _____

3 ___ ___ ___   4 ___ ___ ___ _____

18 **Read aloud. Then listen and check.**

Dad has his dinner. Mum has got a letter. The girl plays with the dog.

19 Read and write *T = True* or *F = False.*

1 Martin has got two classmates. ☐

2 Kenny was born in Glasgow. ☐

3 Roberta is from Jamaica. ☐

4 Roberta has got blond hair. ☐

20 Write about Tanya, her family and friends.

○ Name: Tanya Smith
○ Age: 8
○ Friends: Beth (glasses)
○ and Sammy (long hair)
○ From: Canada
○ Mum from: Scotland
○ Dad from: Canada
○ Grandad from: India

Tanya Smith is [1] _____ years old. Here is Tanya with her family and friends.

Tanya is from [2] _____. Her mum is from [3] _____ and her dad is

from [4] _____. Her grandad is from [5] _____.

Here are Tanya's friends, Sammy and Beth. Sammy has got [6] _____ and

Beth has got [7] _____.

21 Look and match.

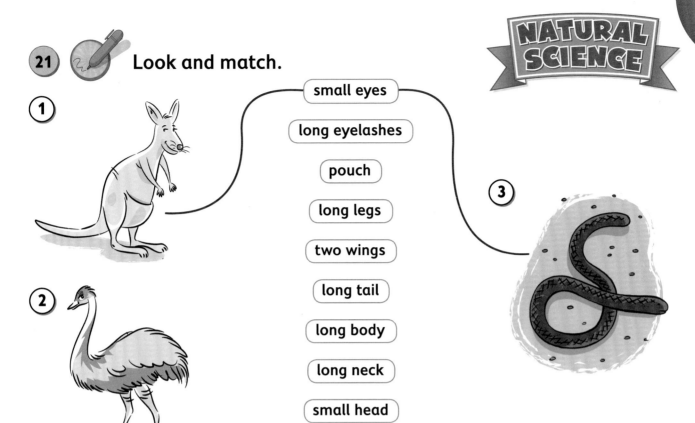

1

2

3

- small eyes
- long eyelashes
- pouch
- long legs
- two wings
- long tail
- long body
- long neck
- small head
- big body

22 Draw a wild animal. Then write.

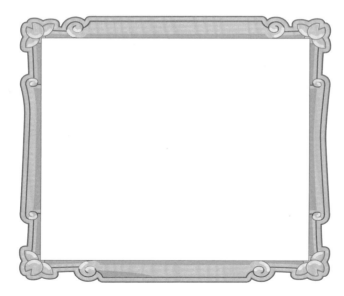

This is a _____.

It's got _____.

It hasn't got _____.

23 **Look and write.**

| moustache | ~~hair~~ | nose | glasses | beard | eyebrows |

1 _____hair_____   2 _____

3 _____   4 _____

5 _____   6 _____

24 **Unscramble and write.**

1 nich _____chin_____   2 sthec _____   3 mahctos _____

4 msra _____   5 hsudolres _____   6 aleeshsey _____

25 **Write. Use the words in Activity 24.**

1 _____She's got_____ long _____
and a round _____.

2 _____ strong _____
and a flat _____.

3 _____ broad _____
and a strong _____.

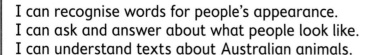

I can recognise words for people's appearance.
I can ask and answer about what people look like.
I can understand texts about Australian animals.

26 **Look and write.**

1

_____ chin _____

2

_____

3

_____

4

_____

5

_____

6

_____

27 **Read and write about yourself.**

1  Have you got a round chin? _____.

2 Have you got a black moustache? _____.

3  Have you got short fingernails? _____.

4 Have you got strong arms? _____.

28 **Write about a friend or family member.**

My _____ has got _____

and _____.

He/She hasn't got _____.

3 Pets

1 Look and write.

| beak | claws | ~~feathers~~ | fins | fur | paws | tail | wings |

1

2

3

4

__feathers__

_____

_____

_____

5

6

7

8

_____

_____

_____

_____

2 Look and write.

| ~~cat~~ | parrot | wings | rabbit | skin | snake | whiskers | paws |

1

We've got a  and a . Our ____cat____ has got long _____.

Our _____ has got green and brown _____.

2

We've got a  and a _____. Our _____ has got white _____.

Our _____ has got two _____ _____.

3 **Look and write.**

1 What _____does_____ it look like? _____It's got_____ two eyes.

_____It hasn't got_____ legs

2 _____ does it _____ like?

_____ a tail. _____ arms.

3 What do _____ look _____?

_____ claws. _____ fur.

4 **Look and write.**

1 The rabbit has got ____paws____ and _____.

2 The parrot has got two _____ and a _____.

3 The cat hasn't got _____.

4 The dog has got _____.

5 The snake hasn't got _____.

6 The frog has got green _____. It hasn't got _____.

7 The fish has got _____.

5 **Listen and draw. Then write.**

1   The tortoise has got a
            _____hard shell_____.

2   The cat has got
            _____.

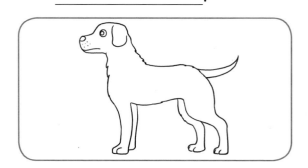

3   The eagle has got

            _____.

4   The dog has got

            _____.

6 **Match.**

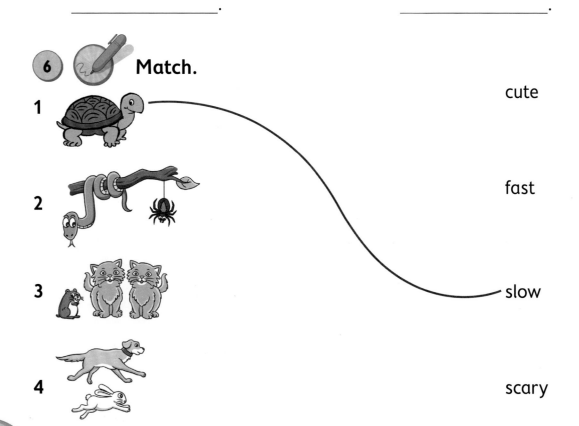

cute

fast

slow

scary

7   **Listen and circle. Then write.**

Animal:	cat / (rabbit)
Name:	Luke / Lily
Age:	3 years old / 8 years old
Colour:	white / brown
Legs:	no legs / four legs
Food:	eggs / vegetables

I've got a pet. It's a [1] __rabbit__ but it doesn't look like a rabbit.

Its name is [2] _____. It's [3] _____ years old. It's [4] _____

and round like a ball. It's got thick, long fur. It's got two eyes and

[5] _____ legs but you can't see them. There's a lot of fur!

It's got a cage with [6] _____, water and toys.

8 **Look at Activity 7 and write.**

What [1] __does it__ look like?
Has it got fins?

[4] _____ a hard shell?

Has it got [7] _____?

[10] _____ is it?

[2] _____, it [3] _____.

[5] _____, it [6] _____.

[8] _____, it [9] _____.
It's thick and long.

It's a [11] _____.

9 Read the story again. What does the wabberjock look like? Write. _____.

10 Look and write.

1

Has it got spots?   <u>Yes, it has</u> .

Has it got a short tail?   _____ .

Has it got sharp teeth?   _____ .

Is it the wabberjock?   _____ .

2

Is it very big?   _____ .

Has it got long legs?   _____ .

Has it got spots?   _____ .

Is it the wabberjock?   _____ .

3

Is it small?   _____ .

Has it got spots?   _____ .

Has it got a long tail?   _____ .

Is it the wabberjock?   _____ .

11 Look at Activity 10 and write.

1 This animal has got blue _____ and spots. It's got a long _____ and sharp _____. It isn't the wabberjock.

2 This animal is very _____. It's got orange fur and _____.
It isn't the wabberjock.

3 This animal has got pink _____ and spots. It's got a _____ tail.
It's the wabberjock!

12 Read the words. Circle the pictures.

~~coin~~ eat leaf tea

13 Listen and connect the letters. Then write.

1:78

1 c   i   k   r ___ ____

2 d   a   ng   c _a_ _p_

3 r   n   p   d ___ ___

4 i   i   g   i ___ ___

14 Listen and write the words.

1:79

1 _p_ _ea_ _ch_   2 ___ ___

3 ___ ___   4 ___ ___ ___

15 Read aloud. Then listen and check.

1:80

Join me for tea. We can have leaf tea in a cup. We can eat too.

Wider World

16 **Read and match.**

1 His name is Charlie. **2** His name is Olly. **3** His name is Fluffy.

4 He's 4 years old. **5** He likes children. **6** He is a good cat.

17  **Draw your favourite animal. Then write.**

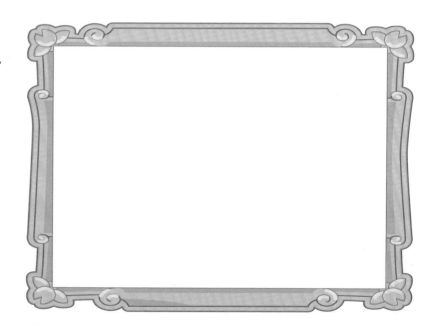

My favourite animal is a _____. It's _____.

It's got _____.

It hasn't got _____.

18 **Number the pictures in order. Then write.**

Life cycle of the butterfly

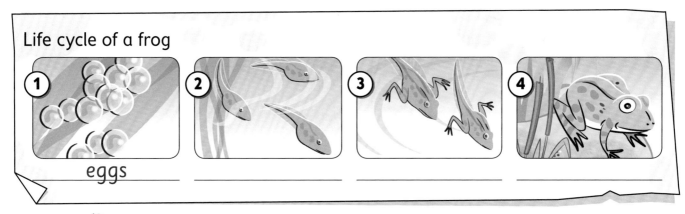

a [ ]   b [1]   c [ ]   d [ ]

| butterflies   caterpillars   cocoons   eggs |

First there are small ____eggs____. Then there are _____.

Then there are _____. Finally, there are _____.

19  **Look and write.**

| big tadpoles   eggs   frogs   small tadpoles |

Life cycle of a frog

1   2   3   4

____eggs____   _____   _____   _____

20 **Read and write.**

1   Have butterflies got wings?   ___Yes, they have___.

2   Have frogs got big mouths?   _____.

3   Have small tadpoles got legs?   _____.

4   Have caterpillars got legs?   _____.

21 **Unscramble and write.**

skewhirs   ginsw   wacsl   sifn   aftershe   swap

1 _____whiskers_____   2 _____

3 _____   4 _____

5 _____   6 _____

  22 **Look and tick (✓).**

	Fast	Slow	Smooth skin	Soft fur	Hard shell
Hamster	✓			✓	
Tortoise					
Frog					

 23 **Look at Activity 22 and write.**

1   The hamster is _____fast_____. It's got _____

but it hasn't got _____.

2   The tortoise is _____. _____.

3   The frog _____. _____.

**I CAN** ———————————

I can identify animal body parts.
I can ask and answer about what animals look like.
I can understand texts about animal life cycles.

24 **Draw and label one animal you like and one animal you don't like.**

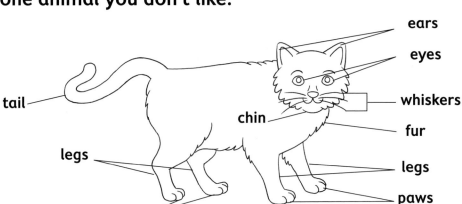

ears

eyes

whiskers

fur

legs

paws

tail

chin

legs

paws

cat

_____   _____

25  **Choose an animal from Activity 24 and write.**

The _____ has got _____ and _____ but it hasn't

got _____.

26 **Write about your favourite pet.**

My favourite pet is a _____. It is _____.

It's got _____ but it hasn't got _____.

4 Home

1 Match.

wardrobe

mirror

plant

picture

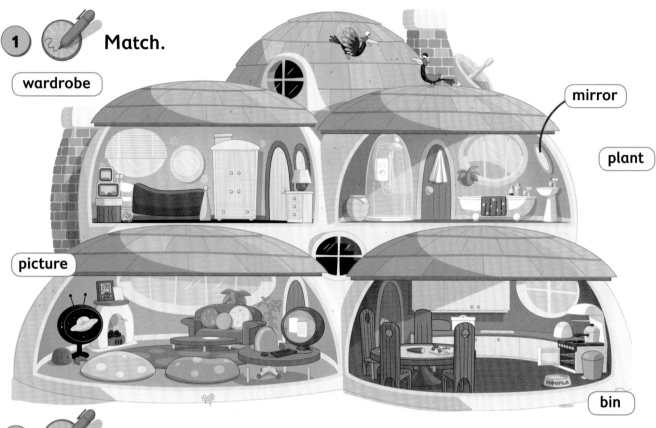

bin

2 Look at Activity 1 and write.

opposite in front of behind above below ~~in front of~~ next to

1 The sofa is _____ in front of _____ the plant.

2 The sofa is _____ the small table.

3 The bin is _____ the cooker.

4 The bath is _____ the window.

5 The mirror is _____ the sink.

6 The wardrobe is _____ the bed.

7 The chair is _____ the cooker.

Read. Then draw the items in the picture.

1   There's a plant in the bathroom. It's opposite the shower.

2   There's a wardrobe in the bedroom. It's next to the bed.

3   There's a lamp in the living room. It's behind the sofa.

4   There's a picture in the kitchen. It's above the sink.

4 **Look at Activity 3 and write T = True or F = False.**

1   There are pictures in the bedroom. They're above the bed   T

2   There's a plant in the living room. It's behind the sofa.

3   There's a bin in the kitchen. It's in front of the fridge.

4   There's a cooker in the kitchen. It's next to the sink.

5   There's a mirror in the bathroom. It's above the sink.

6   There's a lamp in the bedroom. It's next to the bed.

7   There's a frog in the bathroom. It's in the sink.

5 **Look and write.**

blanket   broom   ~~comb~~   cupboard   pans   pots   plates   towels

1   Is the __comb__ on the cooker?   Yes, it is.

2   Are the _____ in the bath?   Yes, they are.

3   Are the _____ in the sink?   No, they aren't. They're on the table.

4   Is the _____ in front of the sofa?   Yes, it is.

5   Are the _____ in the kitchen?   Yes, they are.

6   Are the _____ in the cupboard?   No, they aren't. They're on the sofa.

7   Is the _____ behind the sink?   No, it isn't. It's in front of the TV.

8   Is the _____ in the kitchen?   Yes, it is.

6   **Listen and write.**

1   __Yes__, it __is__.   **2**   ____, they ____.   **3**   ____, it ____.

4   ____, it ____.   **5**   ____, it ____.   **6**   ____, it ____.

7 **Look and write.**

| bed chair computer in front of next to plant sofa under |

1 Is the hamster on the bed? <u>No, it isn't. It's under the bed</u>.

2 Is the hamster in the shower? _____.

3 Is the hamster on the sofa? _____.

4 _____ behind the _____? Yes, it is.

5 _____ in front of the _____? No, it isn't.

It's above the chair.

6 Is the hamster under the computer? _____

_____.

8 **Look at Activity 7. Then listen and write the number.**

a 3   b ☐   c ☐   d ☐   e ☐   f ☐

9 Read the story again. Has Fid got a tifftiff plant? Write. _____.

10 Number the pictures in order. Then write.

It isn't your plant. It's our plant!

Oh, no! My poor kitchen!

Have you got a tifftiff plant?

Oh, no! The trickster's got the tifftiff plant!

got   Have   kitchen   plant

a It isn't your plant. It's our _____!

b Oh, no! My poor _____!

c _____ you got a tifftiff plant?

d Oh, no! The trickster's _____ the tifftiff plant!

11 Where's the tifftiff plant? Look and write.

1 It's _____ the table.   **2** It's _____ the cooker.

3 It's _____ the window.   **4** It's _____ the table.

12 Read the words.
Circle the pictures.

PHONICS
a_e   i_e   o_e

~~bone~~ cake home time

13 Listen and connect the letters. Then write.
2:19

1   k   i   t   t _____ ____

2   t   ee   l   k _i_ ck__

3   k   ai   ck   f _____ ____

4   f   i   d   k ____ ____

14 Listen and write the words.
2:20

1   _w_ ave___   2 _____ _____   3 ____ _____

4   ____ _____   5 ____ _____

15 Read aloud. Then listen and check.
2:21

The boy eats his cake and the dog has got a bone. It's time to go home but the park is fun.

Wider World

16 **Read and match.**

bed

posters

TV

toys

computer

desk

17 **Read and write T = True or F = False.**

What is your bedroom like?

1	It's big.	☐	**2** It's got a small wardrobe.	☐
3	I've got a bunk bed.	☐	**4** I've got a computer.	☐
5	There's a desk.	☐	**6** There's a TV.	☐

18  **Write about your bedroom.**

My bedroom is _____. It's got _____.

I've got _____ in my bedroom.

There's a _____ in my bedroom.

19   **Find and colour the frog.**

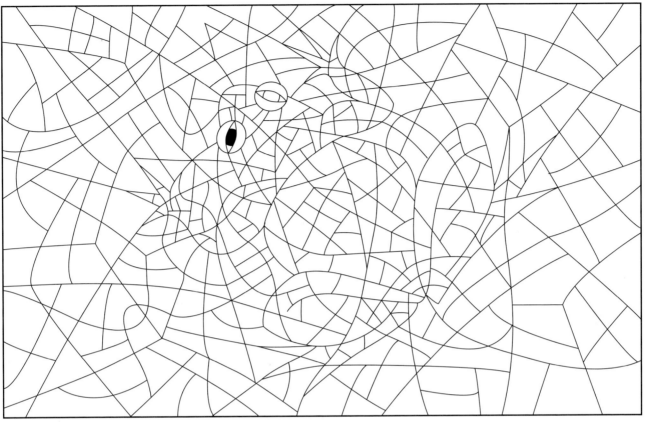

20 **Write. Then draw a mosaic animal.**

square

_____

_____

_____

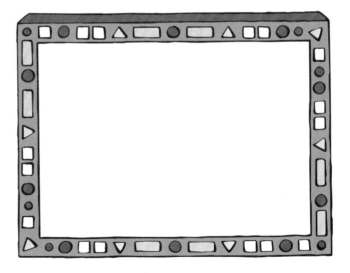

21 **Write three things we can use to make mosaics.**

1 _____ 2 _____ 3 _____

22 Unscramble and write.

1 empcourt _____computer_____ 2 ebrawrdo _____

3 adupborc _____ 4 omorb _____

5 bocm _____ 6 urbshototh _____

7 epalts _____ 8 ewolts _____

9 kenbalts _____ 10 sapn _____

23 Listen and draw. Then write.

1 There are ___towels___ in the bathroom. They're _____ the sink.

2 There's a bed _____ the _____.

3 Is there a lamp behind the sofa? _____.

4 Is there a wardrobe in the bedroom? _____.

5 There are _____ in the living room.
  They're _____ the sofa.

6 Is there a mirror above the sink? _____.

I can identify furniture and household items.
I can say where things are in a room.
I can understand a text about mosaics.

24 **Draw and colour a room in your house.**

25  **Look at Activity 24 and write.**

> My living room is great! There is a big sofa. There is a small table in front of the sofa. There is a big green plant. The TV is opposite the plant. There is a computer on the big table behind the sofa. There are pictures above the computer.

My _____ is _____. There is _____

_____. There is _____.

The _____ is _____ the _____. There is _____

_____. There are _____.

26  **Write questions about your house.**

1   Is there _____ opposite the _____? Yes, there is.

2   Are there _____ above the _____? No, there aren't.

3   _____ below the _____? No, there isn't.

4   _____ in front of the _____? Yes, there is.

5 Clothes

1 Match.

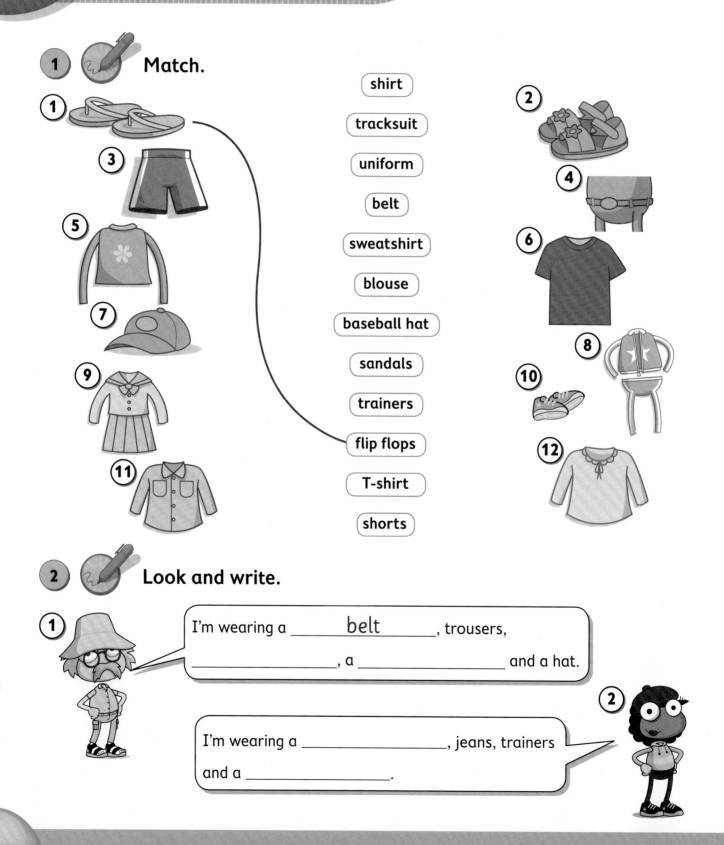

shirt

tracksuit

uniform

belt

sweatshirt

blouse

baseball hat

sandals

trainers

flip flops

T-shirt

shorts

2 Look and write.

1. I'm wearing a _____ belt _____, trousers, _____, a _____ and a hat.

2. I'm wearing a _____, jeans, trainers and a _____.

3   **Listen and draw. Then colour.**

What's he wearing?

He's wearing...

4   **Look at Activity 3 and write.**

1   What's he wearing? He's wearing a ___baseball hat___, a _____,
              _____ and _____.

2   Is he wearing a belt?_____, he _____.

3   Is he wearing a baseball hat? _____, he _____.

5   **Write. Then listen and colour.**

> ~~beanie~~ hiking boots scarf ski jacket tights woolly jumper

1 ___beanie___

2 _____

3 _____

4 _____

5 _____

6 _____

6 **Look at Activity 5 and write.**

> colourful fancy leather plain

1 ___She's___ wearing a _____ ski jacket.

2 _____ wearing a _____ beanie.

3 Is _____ wearing _____ shoes? Yes, _____ .

4 Is _____ wearing a _____ woolly jumper?
No, _____ .

7 **2:38** **Look and tick (✓). Then listen and circle.**

shoes	☐	baseball hat	☐
trainers	✓	belt	☐
blouse	☐	skirt	☐
sweatshirt	☐	jeans	☐
glasses	☐	shorts	☐

1 Yes, she is. / No, she isn't.

2 Yes, she is. / No, she isn't.

3 Yes, she is. / No, she isn't.

4 Yes, she is. / No, she isn't.

8 **Write.**

my favourite   ~~These are~~   I love   This is

1
_____These are_____ my favourite hiking boots. _____ my favourite jumper.

2
_____ my tights and my leather shoes! This is _____ scarf.

9 **Tick (✓) your favourite clothes.**

a baseball hat	☐	a ski jacket	☐	a sweatshirt	☐
a beanie	☐	a blouse	☐	blue jeans	☐
a belt	☐	a uniform	☐	a T-shirt	☐
sandals	☐	flip flops	☐	shorts	☐

10 **Read the story again. Is PROD 2 wearing a red shirt? Write.** _____.

11 **Unscramble and write.**

got He's tifftiff plant. the
_____

1

shirt! at Look red the
_____

2

jeans! the Behind There!
_____

3

a dress. is PROD 2 wearing
_____

4

12 **Look and write.**

~~dress~~   uniform   red glasses

1 Is PROD2 wearing a red shirt? _No, he isn't. He's wearing a dress_ .

2 Is Katy wearing a tracksuit? _____.

3 Is Kim wearing a uniform? _____.

4 Is the red trickster wearing colourful glasses?

_____.

13   Read the words.
Circle the pictures.

~~scarf~~   skate   spoon   star

14 Listen and connect the letters. Then write.
2:43

1 | h | | u | | t | c _____ ____

2 | c | | igh | | t | c _____ ____

3 | l | | oa | | t | h _a_ _t_

4 | c | | a | | p | l _____ ____

15 Listen and write the words.
2:44

1 __sm_ _e_ _ll__   2 _____ ____ __

3 _____ ____ ___   4 _____ ____ ___

16 Read aloud. Then listen and check.
2:45

The cats skate on the lake. One wears a hat and one wears a scarf.

The moon is high and we can see a big star.

Wider World

17 **Read and colour.**

1 My name's Clara and I'm from Mexico. In my school we don't wear a uniform. Here I'm wearing black trousers, a plain red T-shirt and my favourite trainers. They're black and very comfortable.

2 My name's Jiaming. I'm from China. We wear a uniform in my school. I'm wearing blue shorts, a black shirt, grey socks and brown sandals. These are my favourite sandals.

18  **Read and write *T = True* or *F = False*.**

1 Clara is wearing a uniform. ☐ F

2 Clara is wearing her favourite trainers. ☐

3 Clara is not wearing black trousers. ☐

4 Jiaming is wearing shorts. ☐

5 Jiaming is not wearing a uniform. ☐

6 Jiaming is wearing his favourite sandals. ☐

19  **Write about yourself.**

I'm wearing _____.

I'm not wearing _____.

20 Match.

1 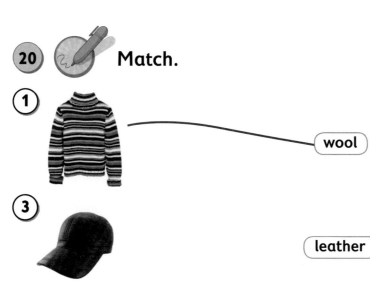 wool

2

3  leather

4

5  cotton

6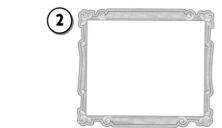

21 Draw four items of clothing. Then write.

1

wool

2

leather

3

cotton

4

polyester

1   The _____ is made from wool.

2   The _____ made from _____.

3   The _____ cotton.

4   The _____.

22   **Look and write.**

| sandals | woolly jumper | beanie | tights | tracksuit | ~~belt~~ | blouse | scarf |

____belt____ _____ _____ _____

_____ _____ _____ _____

23 **Read and write.**

1 Is he wearing trainers?

  No, he isn't. He's wearing hiking boots .

2 _____ ?

  Yes, he is. It's his favourite T-shirt.

3 Is he wearing trousers?

  _____ .

4 _____ ?

  Yes, he is. He loves his baseball hat.

I can identify and describe items of clothing.
I can ask and answer about what people are wearing.
I can understand a text about materials.

24 **Draw and colour your favourite clothes.**

25 **Write about your favourite clothes.**

These are my favourite trainers. They're _____.

This is my favourite baseball hat. It's _____.

I love my _____. _____ fancy.

_____. _____ colourful.

_____. _____ plain.

_____. _____ leather.

26 **Pretend you're wearing your favourite clothes. Write.**

Today I'm wearing _____

_____.

6 Sports

  Look and number.

1	jump	**2**	play basketball	**3**	run	**4**	climb trees
5	ride a bike	**6**	catch a ball	**7**	play badminton	**8**	do taekwondo
9	play football	**10**	play tennis				

 Read and circle for you.

1 I (can / can't) jump.

2 I (can / can't) climb trees.

3 I (can / can't) play badminton.

4 I (can / can't) play football.

5 I (can / can't) play basketball.

6 I (can / can't) ride a bike.

7 I (can / can't) do taekwondo.

8 I (can / can't) play tennis.

9 I (can / can't) run.

10 I (can / can't) catch a ball.

3   **Listen and write ✓ = can or X = can't.**

Paul					✓		
Beth							
Jake							
Gina							
Max							

4 **Look at Activity 3 and write.**

1 Max He can _____ play football _____ but he can't

_____.

2 Beth She can _____ but she can't

_____.

3 Paul _____ but he can't

_____.

4 Jake Can he _____?

No, _____.

5 Gina _____?

Yes, _____.

5 Match the sports and places.

1 basketball court

running track

2

3 bowling alley

swimming pool

4

5 gym

skating rink

6

6 🎧 2:58 Listen and tick (✓).

1 **2** **3**

☐ ✓ | ☐ ☐ | ☐ ☐

7 🎧 2:59 Listen and write ✓ = *was* or ✗ = *wasn't*.

1 running track ☒ **2** basketball court ☐ **3** gym ☐

bowling alley ☐ skating rink ☐ ski slope ☐

8 **Look and write ✓ = can or ✗ = can't.**

 **1** ✓

 **2**

 **3**

 **4**

 **5**

 **6**

 **7**

 **8**

9 **Look at Activity 8. Write _and_ or _but_.**

Monkeys can run ¹ _____and_____ jump ² _____ they can't ride a bike.

They can swim ³ _____ climb trees ⁴ _____ they can't play tennis.

They can skate but they can't play football.

10 **Look at Activity 8 and write.**

1 He wasn't at the bowling alley. He _____was_____ at the
_____running track_____.

2 He _____ at the swimming pool. He _____ at
the _____.

3 He _____ basketball court. He _____
_____.

4  _____ skating rink. _____
_____.

5  _____ ski slope. _____
_____.

11 Read the story again. What can't PROD 1 do? Write. _____ .

12 Look at the story again. Write the things PROD 1 and PROD 2 can and can't do.

catch   fly   ~~play basketball~~   play tennis   ride a bike   run fast   swim

PROD 1	
play basketball	✓
_____	☐
_____	☐
_____	☐

PROD 2	
_____	☐
_____	☐
_____	☐
_____	☐

13 Look at Activity 12 and write.

1   PROD 1 can play basketball but he can't run fast _____ .

2   _____ .

3   _____ .

4   _____ .

14   **Read the words. Circle the pictures.**

bl   fl   gl
pl   sl

flag   glass   sleep   slip

15 **Listen and connect the letters. Then write.**
2:66

1   p   e   k   b _____ ___

2   b   oo   ll   p _u_ _ff_

3   f   u   d   b ____ ____

4   b   oo   ff   f _____ ___

16 **Listen and write the words.**
2:67

1   _bl_ _a_ _ck_   2   ____ ____ ___

3   ____ ____ ___   4   ____ ____ ___

17 **Read aloud. Then listen and check.**
2:68

Look at the ship with the black flag. One man slips.

Look out for that shark!

Wider World

18 **Look and write.**

~~cricket pitch~~   baseball field   a baseball bat and ball
a cricket bat and a ball   a cricket team   a baseball team

1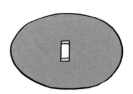

___cricket pitch___

2

_____

3

_____

4

_____

5

_____

6

_____

19 **Look at Activity 18 and write.**

1 This _____pitch_____ is round.

2 A _____ is also called a 'diamond'.

3 You play cricket with _____.

4 You play basketball with _____.

5 A _____ team has got _____ players.

6 A _____ team has got _____ players.

20 **Write about a popular team sport.**

_____ is a popular sport in _____. There are

_____ teams. There are _____ players in each team.

21 **Listen and number.**

 a

 b

 c

 d

 e 1

22 **Make an exercise plan.**

> catch a ball   climb   dance   do taekwondo   play badminton
> play basketball   play football   play tennis   ride my bike   run   swim

My exercise plan

Monday	
Tuesday	
Wednesday	
Thursday	

Friday	
Saturday	
Sunday	

23 **Write about your exercise plan.**

On Monday I can _____, on Tuesday I can _____,

_____

_____

_____ .

24   Look and write ✓ = *can* or ✗ = *can't*.

25 Look at Activity 24 and write.

1 Can Sue play tennis and basketball?

   She can play tennis but she can't play basketball   .

2 Can Lee _____ and _____? _____

   _____.

3 Can Liz _____? _____

   _____.

I CAN

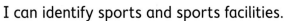

I can identify sports and sports facilities.
I can ask and answer about what people can and can't do.
I can understand fitness instructions.

26 **Write about yourself.**

I can	I can't
_____	_____
_____	_____
_____	_____

27 **Look at Activity 26 and write.**

1 I can _____ but I can't _____.

2 _____.

3 _____.

28 **Unscramble and write the questions. Then write about yourself.**

1 you / trees / can / climb

_____? _____.

2 bike / you / ride / can / a

_____? _____.

7 Food

1 ✏️ **Match.**

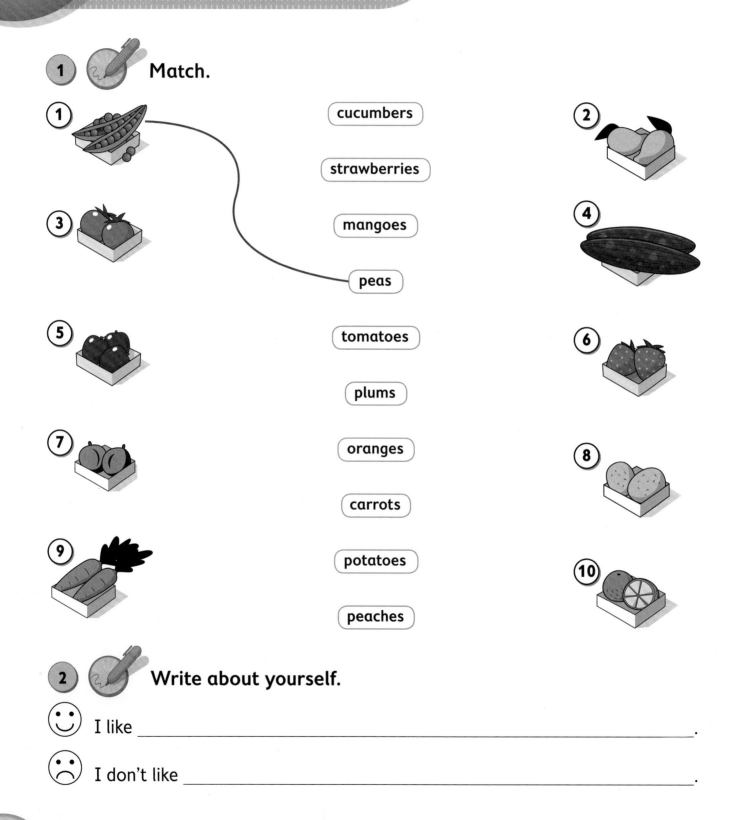

1

cucumbers

2

strawberries

3

mangoes

4

peas

5

tomatoes

6

plums

7

oranges

8

carrots

9

potatoes

10

peaches

2 ✏️ **Write about yourself.**

🙂 I like _____.

🙁 I don't like _____.

3 Listen and write ✓ = *likes* or ✗ = *doesn't like*.

4  Look at Activity 3 and write.

1 Does she like strawberries?

   Yes, she does_____.

2 Does she _____ plums?

   _____.

3 _____ she _____ peas?

   _____.

4 _____ he _____ tomatoes?

_____.

5 _____ cucumbers?

_____.

6 _____ beans?

_____.

5 **Look and write *Y* = *Yes* or *N* = *No*.**

Tim's house		Are there any ...? Is there any ...?		Liz's house
	N	mangoes	Y	
		peaches		
		potatoes		
		strawberries		
		cucumbers		
		watermelon		
		broccoli		
		lettuce		
		chicken		
		cabbage		
		spinach		
		cherries		
		avocados		
		apricots		
		pears		
		papaya		

6   **Look at Activity 5 and write.**

Tim's house

1 Are there any pears?

   No, there aren't_____.

2 Are there any cherries?

   _____.

3 Is there any spinach?

   _____.

Liz's house

1 Is there any watermelon?

   _____.

2 Are there any papayas?

   _____.

3 Is there any cabbage?

   _____.

7   Listen and draw a ☺ or a ☹.

8  Look at Activity 7 and write.

1 Does he like cereal? _Yes, he does_____.

2 Does he like strawberries? _____.

3 Does he like eggs and toast? _____.

4 Does he like peaches? _____.

5 _____ bananas? Yes, he does.

6 _____ avocados? No, he doesn't.

9 Draw food items. Then write.

Fruits

Vegetables

1 Are there any _____? Yes, there are.

2 Is there any _____? No, there isn't.

3 Are there lots of _____?

_____.

4 Is there a lot of _____?

_____.

5 _____? Yes, there are.

6 _____? No, there aren't.

10 Read the story again. What food does Kim like?

Write. _____.

11 Look and write.

1 Does she like eggs?

No, she doesn't _____.

2 Does he like _____?

_____.

3 Is there a tifftiff plant?

_____.

4 Is _____ a tifftiff plant?

_____.

12 Number the pictures in order.

a — I love ...

b — He doesn't like ...!

c — Oh, no!

d — Kim, do you like ...

e — Yuck! No, I don't like ...

13 Read the words.
Circle the pictures.

PHONICS

br cr dr fr
gr pr str tr

~~crab~~ frog string train

14 Listen and connect the letters. Then write.
3:17

1	k	ar	ss	w _____ _____
2	w	i	k	g _____ _____
3	sh	e	l	sh _____ _____
4	g	ir	b	k _i_ _ss_

15 Listen and write the words.
3:18

1 __br__ __ow__ __n__   2 _____ _____ _____

3 _____ _____ _____   4 _____ _____ _____

16 Read aloud. Then listen and check.
3:19

The boy likes his toy train. He can pull it with the string. He's got a green frog, a brown owl and a red crab.

Lesson 6

Wider World

17 Read and write.

 1

I'm Andrea. I'm from Argentina.
I don't like potatoes but I like meat.
My favourite dinner is *asado* or barbecue.
I also like chocolate
sandwiches for a snack.
They aren't healthy but
they are very tasty!

barbecue

pastries

My name's Zeki and I'm from
Turkey. Here, I eat fantastic
pastries with pistachios,
almonds and walnuts. I love
them. I also like chicken and
fruit but I don't like kebabs.

2

1 Does Andrea like barbecue? <u>Yes, she does</u>.

2 Are chocolate sandwiches healthy? _____.

3 Does Zeki like kebabs? _____.

4 Does Zeki like fruit? _____.

18 Write about food from your country.

My name's _____. I'm from _____.

I like _____ but I don't like _____.

My favourite dinner is _____. _____ healthy.

74 **Lessons 7 and 8**

NATURAL SCIENCE

19 **Match.**

1

fruit and vegetables

2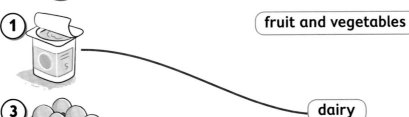

3

dairy

4

5

protein

6

7

fats and sugars

8

9

grains

10

20 **Draw three healthy meals. Use the food groups.**

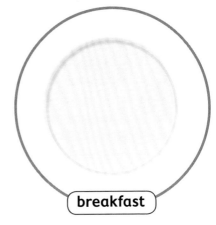

breakfast

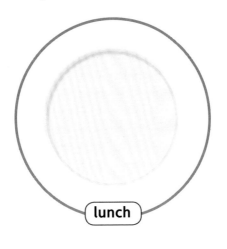

lunch

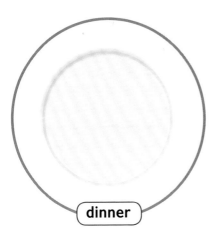

dinner

21 **Look at Activity 20 and write.**

For breakfast, I like _____.

For lunch, I like _____.

For dinner, I like _____.

22 🍕 **Look and write.**

Across →

1

3

5

7

Down ↓

2

4

6

8

¹T O M A T O E S

23 🍕 **Look and write.**

1 Does he like mangoes? _____.

2 _____ strawberries?

_____.

3 Does she like apricots? _____.

4 _____ spinach?

_____.

I CAN

I can identify fruit and vegetables.
I can ask and answer about food likes and dislikes.
I can understand a text about food groups.

24 **Draw food items.**

My fridge	My cupboard

25 **Look at Activity 24 and write.**

1 There is some _____ .

2 There are some _____ .

3 There is a lot of _____ .

4 There are lots of_____ .

5 Is there any cereal? _____ .

6 Are there any strawberries? _____ .

26 **Write about your family.**

My mum likes _____. So do I. She doesn't like _____.

My dad likes _____. Me too. He doesn't _____.

8 Things we do

1 🎧 3:27 **Listen and number.**

a ☐

b ☐

c ☐

d ☐

e ☐

f ☐

g ☐

h ☐

i ☐

2 🖌 **Look at Activity 1 and write.**

cleaning   dancing   doing homework   drinking   sleeping   walking

a _____.   b _____.

d _____.   f _____.

h _____.   i _____.

3 🎧 **3:29** **Listen and match.**

1 climbing a tree · a 🥤

2 drinking juice · b 📘

3 reading a book · c 🎧

4 listening to music · d 🌳

5 cleaning his shoes · e 👟

4 ✏️ **Look at Activity 3 and write.**

1 What are you doing, Captain Conrad? I'm _____.

2 What's Kim doing? _____.

3 _____, Katy? I'm listening to music.

4 What are the PRODs doing? _____.

5 What's the trickster doing? She's _____.

5 **Listen and tick (✓).**

① Marie ☐ Jenny ✓

② Ken ☐ Ben ☐

③ Karl ☐ Jon ☐

④ Kelly ☐ Ann ☐

⑤ Tim ☐ Pete ☐

6  **Look at Activity 5 and write.**

| loudly   playing the piano   playing the violin   quickly |

1 Are you ___playing the piano___, Marie? Yes, I am.

2 Is Ben playing the flute? No, he isn't. He's _____.

3 Is Jon _____ terribly? Yes, he is.

4 Are you playing the trumpet slowly, Ann?

_____.

5 Is Pete singing quietly?

_____.

7 Listen and write.

Hi, Jason!

I'm in Thailand now. I'm having fun but it's very hot!

I'm ¹ __eating__ a sandwich by the pool. My

sister is swimming ² _____ and my mum is

reading ³ _____ . My dad is ⁴ _____

to music and singing ⁵ _____ . But he's funny.

See you soon!

Bye,

Adam

To: Jason Spade
   10 Park Street
   New York
   NY 10013
   United States

8 Look and write.

| playing the piano   quickly   reading   walking |

1 ___Is he___ sleeping?

No, _____ . _____ .

2 Is _____ ?

Yes, _____ .

3 Is _____ slowly?

No, _____ . _____ .

9 Read the story again. Who is helping Hip in the garden? Write. _____.

10 Look and write.

What's she _____?

_____ gardening.

Are they _____ slowly?

No they aren't. They're running _____.

What _____ they doing?

They're going home.

11 Look and write.

listening
going
quietly
flying
reading
sleeping

Captain Conrad's [1] _____ the spaceship. They're [2] _____ home.

Katy's [3] _____ a book about tifftiff plants. Kim's [4] _____ to music.

Is he singing loudly? No, he isn't. He's singing [5] _____. PROD 1 and

PROD 2 are [6] _____.

12   Read the words.
Circle the pictures.

PHONICS

ft   mp   nd   nt
sk   sp   st

~~bump~~   hand   paint   wind

13 Listen and connect the letters. Then write.
3:39

1   qu   e   z   b _____ _____

2   y   i   zz   y _____ ____

3   b   ow   n   qu _i_ _z_

4   d   u   s   d _____ ____

14 Listen and write the words.
3:40

1   _a_ _sk_   2   ____ ____ _____

3   ____ ____ ____   4   ____ ____ _____

15 Read aloud. Then listen and check.
3:41

The painter is up the ladder. The pot goes down with a bump and the paint

goes splat on the man. What a mess!

Wider World

16 Look and write. Then draw and write about yourself.

do yoga   play music   play chess
play tennis   dance

①

_____

② play music

_____

③

_____

④

_____

⑤

_____

⑥

After school, I

_____.

17 Ask your partner about after-school clubs. Then circle.

After-school clubs

What after-school club do you like?

I like tennis / football.

I like dancing / playing chess.

18 **Look and write.**

 NATURAL SCIENCE

fly quickly   colourful   ~~fly slowly~~   hasn't got wings
very big   fly quietly   fly above the clouds   fly into space

1

2

It's flying slowly   .

_____ .

_____ .

_____ .

_____ .

_____ .

_____ .

_____ .

19 **Draw your favourite flying machine. Then write.**

My favourite flying machine is a _____ .

A _____ is _____ .

It _____ wings. It flies _____ .

It can fly _____ .

20 Look and write.

¹ S W I M M I N G

What is the secret word? s _ _ _ _ _ _ _ _ _ _ _ _

21 Look and write.

1 I'm playing the piano ____.

2 ____.

3 ____.

4 ____.

I CAN

I can identify activities and describe how you do them.
I can ask and answer about what people are doing.
I can understand texts about flying machines.

22 **Look and write.**

Talent Show

Anna

Sandy and Amy

Dan

Eddie

Mike and Fred

Gigi

1 What's Eddie doing?   <u>He's playing the trumpet</u>   .

2 What are Sandy and Amy doing?   _____.

3 What's Anna doing?   _____.

4 What are Mike and Fred doing?   _____.

5 What's Dan doing?   _____.

6 What's Gigi doing?   _____.

23 **Draw yourself at a talent show. Then write.**

| slowly   quickly   terribly   loudly   quietly |

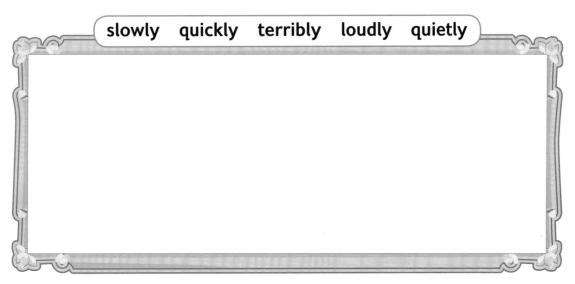

I'm _____.

Goodbye

1 Find and circle the one that doesn't belong. Then write.

1   a   b   c   _thick eyebrows_

2   a   b   c   _____

3   a   b   c   _____

4   a   b   c   _____

5   a   b   c   _____

6   a   b   c   _____

7   a   b   c   _____

8   a   b   c   _____

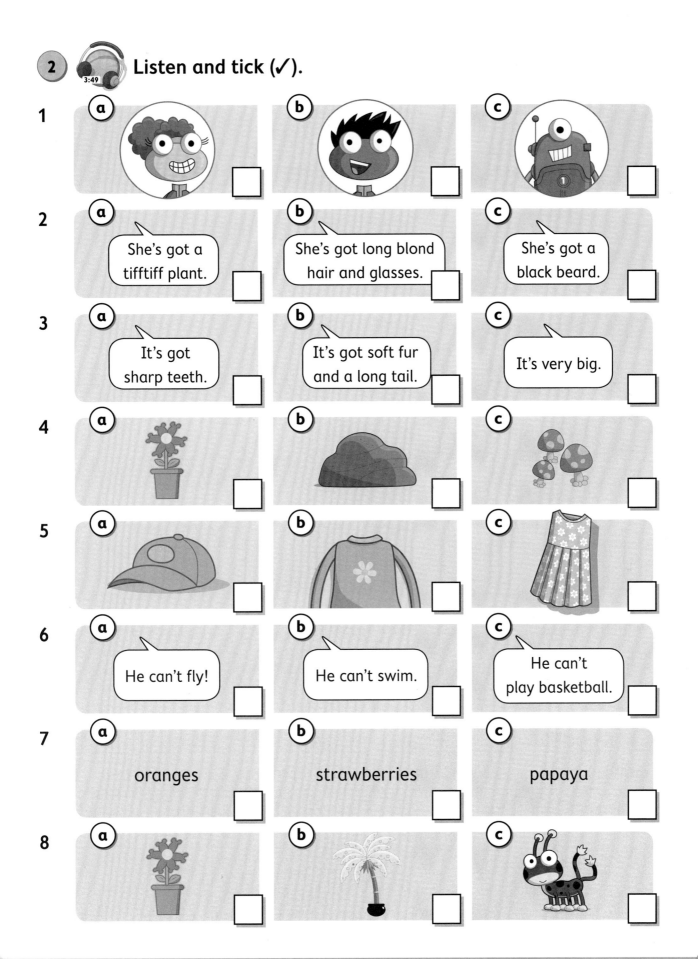

2 🎧 3:49 **Listen and tick (✓).**

1 a b c

2 a She's got a tifftiff plant. b She's got long blond hair and glasses. c She's got a black beard.

3 a It's got sharp teeth. b It's got soft fur and a long tail. c It's very big.

4 a b c

5 a b c

6 a He can't fly! b He can't swim. c He can't play basketball.

7 a oranges b strawberries c papaya

8 a b c

3 **Look and write.**

There is a rainbow _____ .

_____ .

_____ .

There are _____ .

_____ .

_____ .

4 **Listen and tick (✓). Then write.**
3:50

 ☐    ☐   ☐

This is Pauli, my pet ¹ _____. It's got colourful ² _____

and a sharp ³ _____. It's got two ⁴ _____ wings. It can fly

high in the sky. It's got sharp ⁵ _____. Be careful!

5 **Write things that are in your house.**

Bedroom	Bathroom	Living room	Kitchen
bed			

6 **Write about a friend or family member.**

He/She can …	He/She can't …
1 _____ .	1 _____ .
2 _____ .	2 _____ .
3 _____ .	3 _____ .

 7 **Look and write.**

___drinking___   _____   _____   _____

  8 **Choose and write.**

I like _____

and _____ .

I don't like _____

and _____ .

My friend likes _____

and _____ .

My friend doesn't like _____

and _____ .

1 Find, circle and write the Halloween words.

1 _____pumpkin_____

2 _____

3 _____

4 _____

5 _____

6 _____

7 _____

p	m	u	h	p	p	w	b	h	d	t
t	t	e	w	n	s	e	t	e	m	h
t	n	p	i	t	p	k	s	p	i	a
i	m	h	t	m	b	b	h	t	d	t
c	h	b	c	b	t	a	t	k	h	m
h	t	g	h	o	s	t	e	h	m	h
o	g	t	t	s	p	e	h	t	a	u
p	u	m	p	k	i	n	t	o	r	m
t	o	t	o	i	d	n	g	m	i	o
r	t	i	t	r	e	a	i	a	t	o
b	s	t	t	b	r	o	o	m	w	c

 2 Look and write.

1 There _____is_____ _____one_____ ghost.

2 There _____ _____ witches.

3 There are _____ spiders and _____ bats.

4 There are five _____ and six _____ .

Christmas Day

1 Find, circle and write the Christmas words.

1   Christmas tree

2

3

4

5

6

7

c	c	h	o	c	o	l	a	t	e	i	l	n
h	l	i	g	h	t	s	c	o	t	o	r	n
c	m	s	l	r	m	g	t	m	i	c	a	h
k	s	h	c	i	h	c	s	h	c	p	r	g
c	h	r	i	s	t	m	a	s	t	r	e	e
h	e	o	r	t	s	k	r	e	d	e	t	h
c	t	h	c	m	o	s	r	c	s	s	r	c
e	c	c	o	a	s	k	c	s	r	e	a	e
d	t	e	t	s	t	o	c	k	i	n	g	s
t	h	t	e	c	h	s	w	e	e	t	s	n
a	i	r	s	a	s	h	o	c	s	k	m	t
s	e	g	c	r	r	o	d	r	r	m	s	t
l	t	i	r	d	e	t	s	i	a	s	k	m

2 Draw a Christmas tree. Then write.

1	Draw the Christmas tree.	2	Draw presents for your family.
3	Draw lights and sweets on your tree.	4	Colour it.

My tree has got ____lights____ and _____.

There are some _____ for my family.

1 Find and colour.

> eggs = brown   lollipops = red   baskets = yellow
> bonnets = green   bunny = orange.

2 Count and write.

1 There are _____seven_____ eggs.

2 _____ bonnets.

3 _____ lollipops.

4 _____ bunny.

3 Make an Easter card.

1 Decorate the egg.
2 Colour it.
3 Write Happy Easter!

April Fools' Day

1  **Find, circle and write the April Fools' Day words.**

1 surprise

2 _____

3 _____

4 _____

5 _____

u	s	u	r	p	r	i	s	e	i
f	k	r	j	r	f	e	n	i	s
i	r	j	a	j	o	k	e	p	r
f	f	l	t	k	o	i	l	u	k
o	a	p	r	i	l	r	n	r	e
u	s	p	i	e	n	u	i	e	r
l	o	r	b	o	i	f	r	k	i
o	s	o	k	l	s	u	r	o	r
j	k	o	a	u	p	n	j	l	o
c	c	l	o	j	k	t	o	l	o

2 **Read and write.**

Come to the party!

1st April

3 pm

Wear a funny hat.

Wear funny clothes.

Sam

Come _____

_____

_____

_____

_____

_____

Tip!

Use a mirror to read this.

Welcome and Unit 1

1 Read and write about yourself.

1 What's your name? _____.

2 How old are you? _____.

3 What's your favourite day? _____.

4 When were you born? _____.

2 Write.

1	2	3	4	5	6	7	8	9	
11	12	13	14		16		18	19	20
21	22	23	24	25		27		29	30
31		33	34	35	36	37	38		40
	42		44	45	46	47	48	49	50

3 Look and write.

1 Where is he?

At _____

_____ .

2 Where is the cat?

_____

_____ .

4 Write.

| flower birds wind insects butterflies tree ~~rainbow~~ spiders |

There's ...

1 _____ a rainbow _____ .

2 _____ .

There are ...

1 _____ .

2 _____ .

96   Unit 1 Extra practice

Unit 2

1 Write the words in alphabetical order.

> eyes   moustache   hair   nose   mouth
> glasses   ~~beard~~   stomach   chin

1 _____beard_____   2 _____   3 _____

4 _____   5 _____   6 _____

7 _____   8 _____   9 _____

2 Write about yourself.

> nose   hair   eyes   eyebrows   glasses   shoulders   fingernails   neck

I've got ...   I haven't got ...

1 _____blue eyes_____ .   1 _____a long neck_____ .

2 _____ .   2 _____ .

3 _____ .   3 _____ .

3 Write about your teacher.

1 He/She has got _____ .

2 He/She hasn't got _____ .

4 Ask your partner the questions. Then write.

1 Have you got brown eyes?   _____ .

2 Have you got red hair?   _____ .

3 Have you got a small nose?   _____ .

4 Have you got thick eyebrows?   _____ .

Unit 3

1 Write about an animal.

> wings   stripy   fur   soft   claws   feathers   skin
> wings   whiskers   spotty   shell   hard   sharp

It's got ...

1 _____ a hard shell _____ .

2 _____ .

3 _____ .

4 _____ .

It hasn't got ...

1 _____ spotty wings _____ .

2 _____ .

3 _____ .

4 _____ .

2 Read and write about yourself.

1   Have you got a cat?   _____ .

2   Have you got a dog?   _____ .

3   Have you got a tortoise?   _____ .

4   Have you got a bird?   _____ .

3 Draw an animal. Then write.

It's got _____

_____ .

It hasn't got _____

_____ .

Unit 4

1 Write about your house.

> there's   there isn't   there are   there aren't any

1   In my bedroom _____ a wardrobe.

2   In my bathroom _____ pots.

3   In my kitchen _____ plants.

4   In my living room _____ a comb.

2 Ask your partner about their house.
Write questions and answers.

1   Is there a _____ mirror _____ in your _____ bathroom _____?

_____.

2   Is _____?   _____.

3   Are _____?   _____.

4   Are _____?   _____.

3 Draw a room. Then write.

> in front of   behind   next to   above   below   opposite

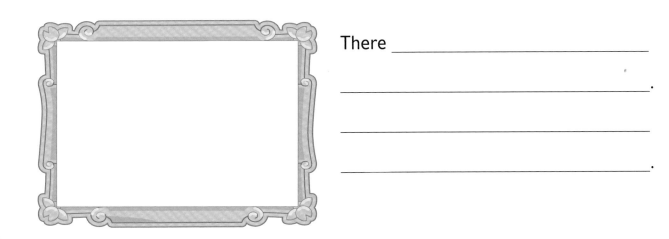

There _____

_____.

_____

_____.

Unit 5

1 Write clothes words.

1 ___blouse___   2 _____   3 _____

4 _____   5 _____   6 _____

7 _____   8 _____   9 _____

2 Write about yourself and a friend.

I'm wearing _____ and _____.

My friend is wearing _____ and _____.

3 Read and write about yourself.

1 Are you wearing a T-shirt?   _____.

2 Are you wearing a belt?   _____.

3 Are you wearing shorts?   _____.

4 Are you wearing a uniform?   _____.

4 Draw your favourite clothes. Then write.

1 This is my favourite _____
_____.

2 These are my favourite _____
_____.

Unit 6

1   **Unscramble and write.**

1 mujp ___jump___ 2 tsenni _____ 3 ceabh _____

4 iudstam _____ 5 myg _____ 6 urn _____

7 ypal bofotall 8 miclb eerts 9 od adokwonet

_____ _____ _____

2   **Write about yourself.**

I can ...   I can't ...

1 _____.   1 _____.

2 _____.   2 _____.

3 **Ask your partner about their abilities. Then write.**

He/She can ...   He/She can't ...

1 _____.   1 _____.

2 _____.   2 _____.

4 **Look and write.**

1   2

He   He   She   She

___wasn't at the___ _____ _____ _____

___basketball___   _____ _____ _____

___court___.   _____. _____. _____.

Unit 7

1 **Write the words in alphabetical order.**

| potatoes   tomatoes   cucumbers   strawberries   plums   ~~apricots~~ |

1 _____apricots_____   2 _____   3 _____

4 _____   5 _____   6 _____

2 **Read and write about yourself.**

1   Do you like peas?   _____.

2   Do you like beans?   _____.

3   Do you like tomatoes?   _____.

4   Do you like oranges?   _____.

3 **Read and write.**

1   _Do you like carrots?_____? Yes, I like carrots.

2   _____? No, I don't like plums.

3   _____? No, I don't like papaya.

4   _____? Yes, I do. I love cherries.

4 **Look and write.**

1   Is there any broccoli?   _Yes, there is_____.

2   Are there any peas?   _____.

3   Is there any lettuce?   _____.

4   Are there any cucumbers?   _____.

Unit 8

1 ✏️ **Read and write.**

1 <u>What are you doing?</u> ? I'm reading.

2 _____ ? He's sleeping

3 _____ ? No, I'm not listening to music.

4 _____ ? Yes, she's reading quietly.

2 ✏️ **Read and write.**

1 Is he drinking? No, <u>he isn't</u> _____ .

2 Are you playing the violin? Yes, _____ .

3 Is she playing the trumpet? Yes, _____ .

4 Are you cleaning? No, _____ .

3 ✏️ **Imagine and write.**

| doing homework   singing   playing the piano   playing the trumpet |
| playing the flute   terribly   loudly   quickly   slowly   quietly |

1 I <u>'m singing loudly</u> _____ .

2 We _____ .

3 She _____ .

4 They _____ .

5 He _____ .

Picture dictionary

Unit 1
Nature

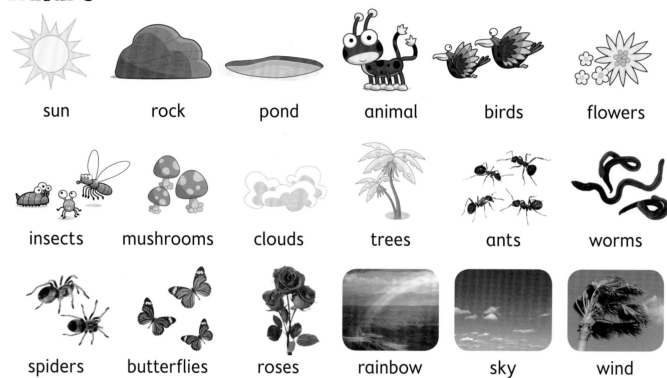

| sun | rock | pond | animal | birds | flowers |

| insects | mushrooms | clouds | trees | ants | worms |

| spiders | butterflies | roses | rainbow | sky | wind |

Places

| library | park | museum | playground |

Maths

| plus | minus | equals |

Unit 2

Describing your body

small nose

black moustache

short beard

brown eyes

thick eyebrows

small glasses

red hair

grey hair

blond hair

round chin

strong chest

flat stomach

broad shoulders

strong arms

long eyelashes

long neck

short fingernails

Australian animals

marsupial

reptile

bird

Unit 3

Animal body parts

tail   beak   wings   feathers   claws

fins   paws   whiskers   skin   fur

Animal characteristics

spotty   stripy   soft   smooth   hard

sharp   cute   scary   fast   slow

Life cycle

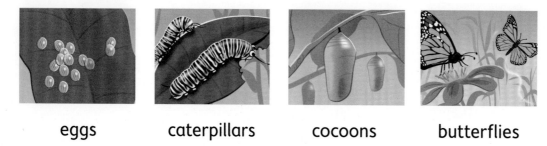

eggs   caterpillars   cocoons   butterflies

Unit 4
Furniture/Household items/Parts of the house

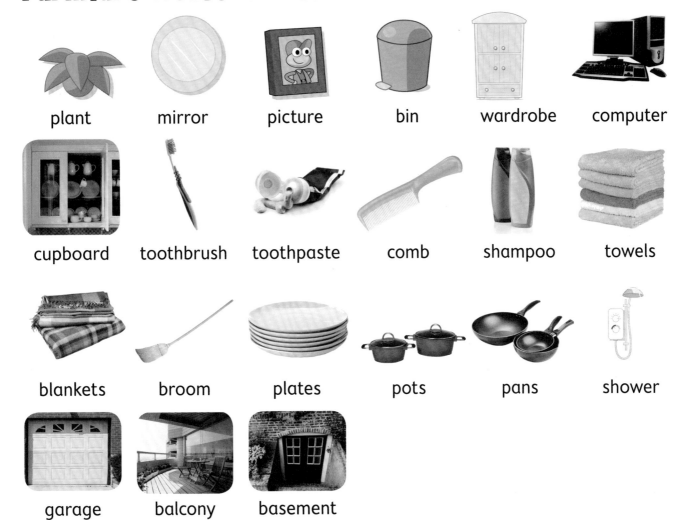

plant   mirror   picture   bin   wardrobe   computer

cupboard   toothbrush   toothpaste   comb   shampoo   towels

blankets   broom   plates   pots   pans   shower

garage   balcony   basement

Prepositions

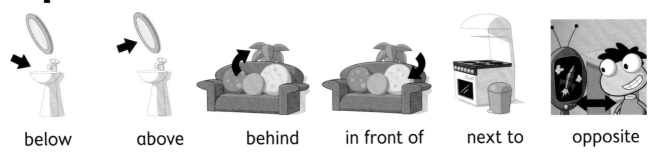

below   above   behind   in front of   next to   opposite

Materials/Shapes

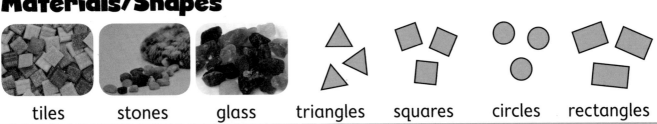

tiles   stones   glass   triangles   squares   circles   rectangles

Unit 5

Clothes

baseball hat   belt   sweatshirt   tracksuit   blouse   uniform

T-shirt   shorts   sandals   flip flops   trainers   shirt

scarf   beanie   ski jacket   woolly jumper   tights   hiking boots

Style

fancy   plain   colourful

Materials

wool   leather   cotton   polyester

Unit 6

Sports

run

ride a bike

catch a ball

play football

jump

climb trees

play tennis

play basketball

play badminton

do taekwondo

Sports facilities

gym

basketball court

running track

stadium

skating rink

ski slope

bowling alley

beach

swimming pool

football pitch

Actions

stretch your arms up

bend your knees

twist your body to the left/right

turn around

Unit 7

Food

peas

mangoes

carrots

cucumbers

plums

oranges

peaches

potatoes

tomatoes

strawberries

beans

broccoli

lettuce

spinach

cabbage

pears

apricots

avocados

cherries

watermelon

papaya

Food groups

fats and sugars

dairy

protein

grains

fruit and vegetables